Rough, Tough Wheels

by Debora Pearson
illustrations by Chum McLeod

Annick Press Ltd.
Toronto • New York • Vancouver

**For my son, Benjamin
—D.P.**

© 2000 Debora Pearson (text)
© 2000 Chum McLeod (illustrations)
Cover design by Sheryl Shapiro.

Annick Press Ltd.
All rights reserved. No part of this work covered by the copyrights hereon may be reproduced or used in any form or by any means – graphic, electronic, or mechanical – without the prior written permission of the publisher.

We acknowledge the support of the Canada Council for the Arts, the Ontario Arts Council, and the Government of Canada through the Book Publishing Industry Development Program (BPIDP) for our publishing activities.

Cataloging in Publication Data
Pearson, Debora
    Rough, tough wheels

(Mighty wheels series)
ISBN 1-55037-637-3 (bound) ISBN 1-55037-636-5 (pbk.)

1. Trucks – Juvenile literature. I. McLeod, Chum. II. Title.
III. Series: Pearson, Debora. Mighty wheels series.

TL230.15.P423 2000   j629.225   C00-930198-4

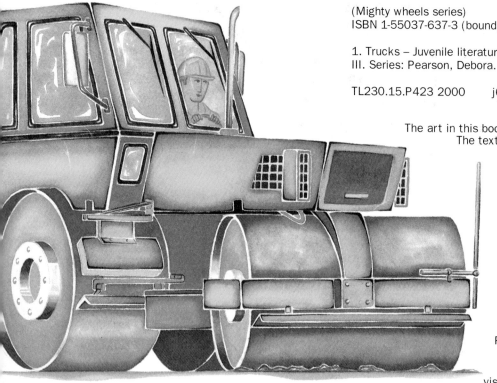

The art in this book was rendered in watercolors.
The text was typeset in Franklin Gothic.

Distributed in Canada by:
Firefly Books Ltd.
3680 Victoria Park Avenue
Willowdale, ON
M2H 3K1

Published in the U.S.A. by:
Annick Press (U.S.) Ltd.
Distributed in the U.S.A. by:
Firefly Books (U.S.) Inc.
P.O. Box 1338, Ellicott Station
Buffalo, NY 14205

Printed and bound in Canada by
Friesens, Altona, Manitoba.

visit us at: **www.annickpress.com**

Have you ever gazed at a grader smoothing a dirt road or seen an excavator tear down a house while in the company of a toddler or preschooler? If you have, then you probably know how young children feel about these machines. They're big, loud creatures on wheels — lively, powerful, and wonderful to watch!

Looking at motor vehicles and talking about them are some of the simplest forms of entertainment around. They're also great ways to share basic ideas and concepts with young children. As you travel through this book, you can talk about what goes up and what goes down, what moves quickly and what moves slowly, what's at the front of a particular vehicle and what's at the back of it. Together you can compare the way a car looks before it goes in the car crusher with the way a car looks after it comes out, and you can make up your own sound effects when you come to the monster trucks and the paver. It's all roaring good fun, and it's waiting for you inside *Rough, Tough Wheels.*

Snorting, snarling monster trucks leap and wheel before a crowd. People cheer, big trucks roar.

**What's that whimper? What's that moan?
A monster truck has broken down.**

A tow truck lugs it to the garage where it will be fixed.

A car crusher crumples worn-out
cars as if they were made of paper.

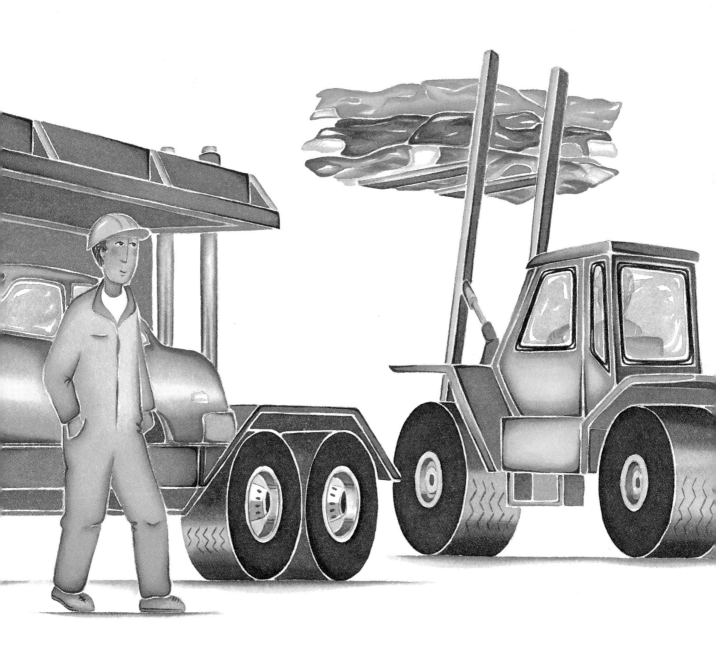

**The flattened slabs it leaves behind
are melted down to make new things.**

An excavator sinks its jaws into a house and tears it apart.

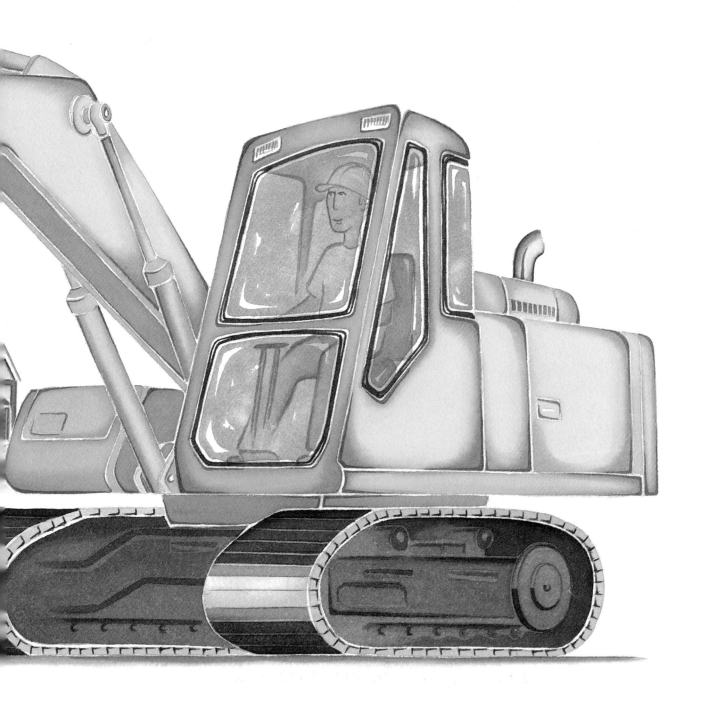

**The mighty dolly on this truck
can hold a house and haul it too.**

A tree spade thrusts its long,
sharp blades into the ground

and scoops out dirt. Then it picks up a
tree and plants it in the deep, wide hole.

After trees have been cut down, a log loader claws them

off the ground and stacks them on the logging truck.

**A grader rumbles over earth and scrapes
it with a blade. The smooth dirt road the
grader makes will soon be paved.**

A paver swallows asphalt in its hopper at the front. Then the big machine crawls along and

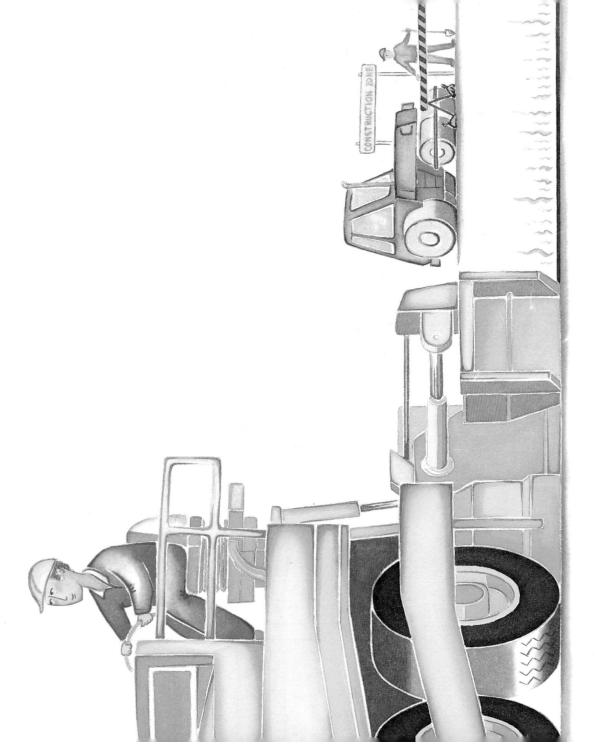

oozes out its heated load. Now the road is coated with a steamy, sticky top.

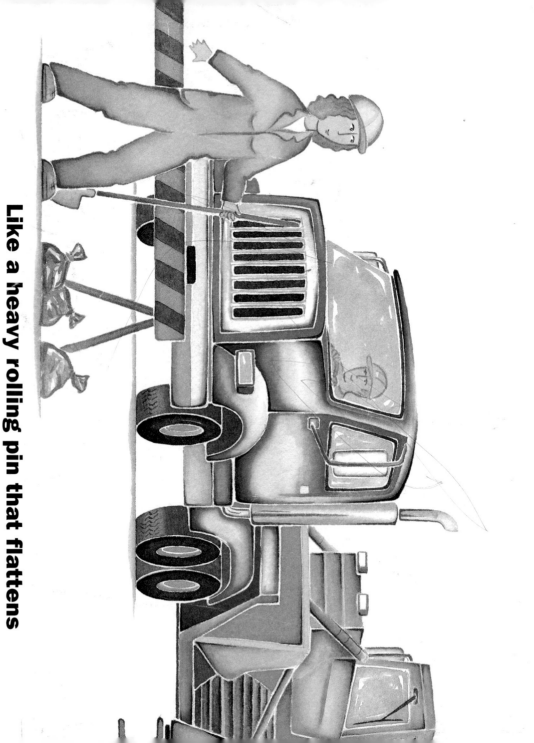

Like a heavy rolling pin that flattens cookie dough, a roller presses on the asphalt while it's soft and warm.

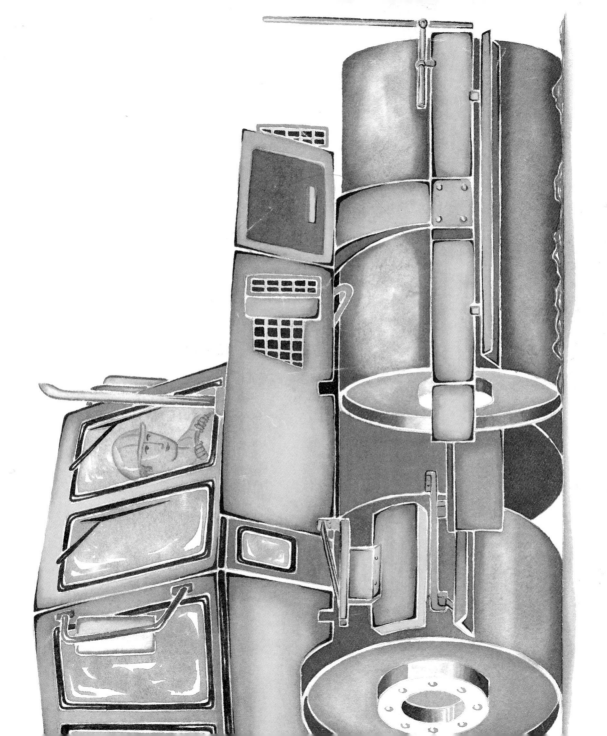

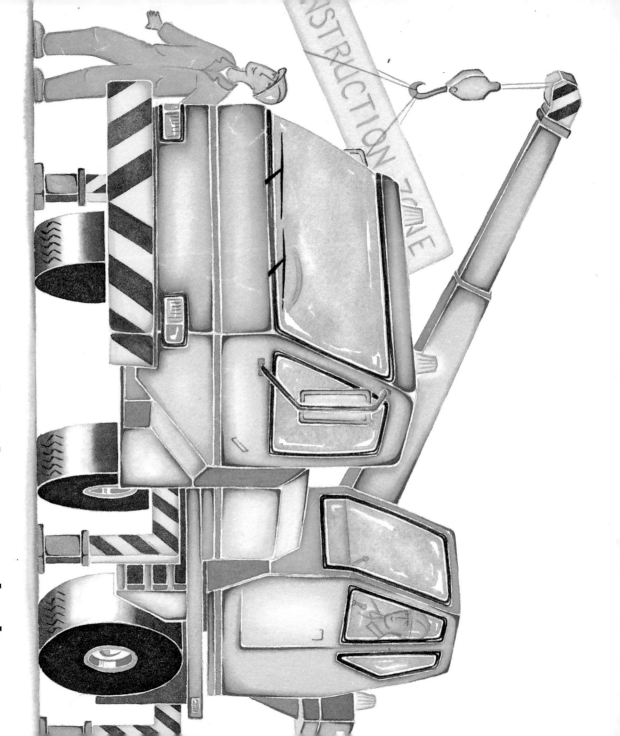

At last the road is ready and a crane unhooks the sign. Rough, tough wheels have done their work – now it's time to drive away.